DATE DUE *7-05*

Robert Goddard

ROCKET MAN

by
Russell Roberts

P.O. Box 196
Hockessin, Delaware 19707
Visit us on the web: www.mitchelllane.com
Comments? email us: mitchelllane@mitchelllane.com

Mitchell Lane
PUBLISHERS

Printing   1   2   3   4   5   6   7   8   9

A Robbie Reader

Hillary Duff	Thomas Edison	Albert Einstein
Philo T. Farnsworth	Henry Ford	**Robert Goddard**
Mia Hamm	Tony Hawk	LeBron James
Donovan McNabb	Dr. Seuss	Charles Schulz

Library of Congress Cataloging-in-Publication Data
Roberts, Russell, 1953-
         Robert Goddard / Russell Roberts.
                  p. cm. — (A Robbie reader)
         Includes bibliographical references and index.
                  ISBN 1-58415-304-0 (library bound)
         1. Goddard, Robert Hutchings, 1882-1945 — Juvenile literature. 2. Rocketry — United States — Biography — Juvenile literature.   I. Title. II. Series.
TL781.85.G6R65 2004
629.4′092--dc22
                                                                                                2004009306

ABOUT THE AUTHOR: Russell Roberts has written and published books on a variety of subjects, including *Ten Days to a Sharper Memory, Discover the Hidden New Jersey,* and *Stolen! A History of Base Stealing.* He also wrote *Pedro Menendez de Aviles* and *Philo T. Farnsworth: The Life of Television's Forgotten Inventor* for Mitchell Lane. He lives in Bordentown, New Jersey with his family and a remarkably lazy, yet fiesty calico cat named Rusti.

PHOTO CREDITS: Cover: Getty Images; p. 4 Getty Images; p. 6 Globe Photos, Inc.; p. 8 Science Photo Library; p. 10 NASA/Mark Marten; p. 12 Archive Photos; p. 14 Getty Images; p. 16 Esther Goddard/Getty Images; p. 18 Getty Images; p. 20 Archive Photos; p. 22 Getty Images; p. 24 Getty Images; p. 26 Barbara Marvis; p. 28 Barbara Marvis, p. 29 J. R. Eyerman/Getty Images

ACKNOWLEDGMENTS: The following story has been thoroughly researched, and to the best of our knowledge, represents a true story. While every possible effort has been made to ensure accuracy, the publisher will not assume liability for damages caused by inaccuracies in the data, and makes no warranty on the accuracy of the information contained herein. This story has not been authorized nor endorsed by anyone associated with Robert Goddard's estate.

TABLE OF CONTENTS

Chapter One
An Unforgettable Day 5

Chapter Two
Young Dreamer 9

Chapter Three
The First Liquid Fuel Rocket 15

Chapter Four
Going Higher and Faster 19

Chapter Five
World War II and Final Years 25

Chronology 30
Find Out More 31
Glossary 32
Index 32

Robert Goddard, around age 50.

AN UNFORGETTABLE DAY

On October 19, 1899, seventeen-year-old Robert Goddard climbed a cherry tree to trim it. He cut off some dead branches. Then he stopped. His thoughts turned to the sky as he looked up.

He thought about building a rocket that would travel into outer space. He wanted to build a rocket that would go to Mars.

No one had ever done that before. Rockets and space travel were in stories, and most people thought rockets were just for books and fireworks. But Robert had studied science. He knew outer space was real. He knew Mars was a real planet.

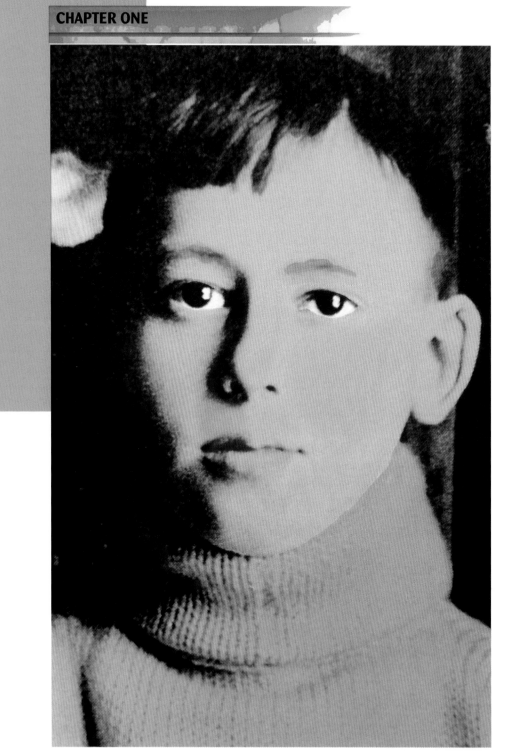

Robert as a young boy.

In the cherry tree, Robert could clearly imagine this space travel. As he climbed down, he was very excited.

Robert never forgot this day for the rest of his life. He called it Anniversary Day. Every year, he marked it as a special day in his diary. He took many photographs of the cherry tree. It was the day that rockets became his life's work.

This is H. G. Wells, author of *War of the Worlds.* Robert liked to read his stories as a child.

YOUNG DREAMER

Robert Hutchings Goddard was born on October 5, 1882, in Worcester (WUSS-ter), Massachusetts. His parents were Nahum and Fannie Goddard.

His mother and grandmother worried about Robert getting sick. They kept him home from school a lot. While he was home, he liked to read. One story he read was called *War of the Worlds* by H. G. Wells. It was about **Martians** (MARSH-ins) invading Earth. The Martians traveled by rockets. Robert's father also read to him from science magazines.

Robert wrote about rockets in notebooks and he built models. Sometimes he got excited, but sometimes he was upset. He thought

After college, Robert became a teacher.

people might be right. Maybe space travel was just for stories. After high school, when so many of his models had failed, he burned all his notebooks.

But he could not forget about rockets.

Robert went to college. They did not have courses about rockets, so he took general science courses instead. After college, he became a teacher. He also worked on rockets. He tried to figure out what kind of **fuel** would make a rocket go fast enough to escape gravity. Gravity is what holds objects on the ground. **Gasoline** (gas-oh-LEEN), a fuel used in cars, cannot make a rocket go fast enough to escape gravity.

In 1913 Robert got a **disease** (diz-EEZE) in his lungs called **tuberculosis** (too-ber-kyew-LOW-sis). It made it hard for him to breathe. The doctors said he would die but Robert fought to get better. He slept on his parents' porch in the winter, breathing in the cold air. It was his own idea of how he could get well.

Robert and one of his rockets.

Robert took long walks to exercise his lungs. Slowly he got better.

By the spring of 1914, Robert was almost completely well again. But his illness had caused him to lose almost all of his hair. He also had lost a lot of weight. He now weighed only 134 pounds. His clothes did not fit very well because he had lost so much weight.

The doctors were surprised he was better. But Robert was not surprised. He believed he could get better, and he did. He also believed that he could build rockets to go into outer space. Now he began trying to prove that belief.

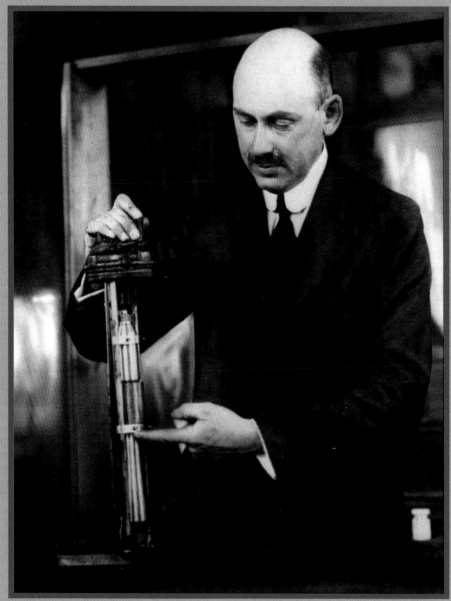

Here Robert points to a model of one of his rockets.

THE FIRST LIQUID FUEL ROCKET

Rockets had been around for almost a thousand years. The Chinese used rockets for fireworks. The British used them as weapons. Robert studied these Earth-bound rockets. He examined different types. How did they work? He looked at their shape and their size. Some rockets used gunpowder for fuel. That would not work for Robert. Gunpowder would not make his rocket fly fast or high enough.

During World War I, Robert worked for the United States military. He wanted to invent a portable rocket weapon that could shoot rockets very far. But the war ended before he could finish. In December 1919, Robert wrote a scientific essay about rockets. He said they might reach the moon.

Robert is about to launch the first liquid fuel rocket. This is the picture taken by his wife, Esther, before the launch.

Newspapers liked that idea. They wrote stories about moon rockets. People who read the stories got excited. They wanted to ride the moon rocket. Rocket clubs were formed. Robert became famous. They called him the Rocket Man.

Robert allowed an honors student named Esther Kisk (es-TER kissk) to help him with his paperwork. Five years later, on June 21, 1924, they were married.

Robert finally found a rocket fuel that would work for him. It was called liquid **oxygen** (ocks-ih-JIN). But it was expensive.

On March 16, 1926, Robert tested a rocket that used gasoline and liquid oxygen. It was a cold day. Snow was on the ground, and Robert could see his breath. Esther took his picture with the rocket.

The liquid oxygen worked. The rocket flew for almost three seconds. It flew 41 feet high. That was the first liquid fuel rocket.

Robert was happy. The picture Esther took became famous.

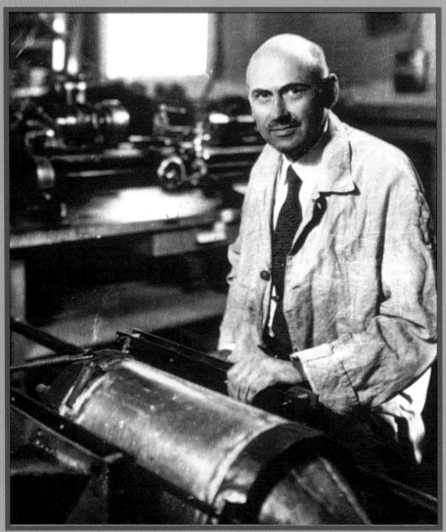

This is Robert with one of his best rockets. This rocket went faster than the speed of sound.

GOING HIGHER AND FASTER

Robert's next rockets were bigger, and they went higher and faster. One went almost 100 feet and then exploded. The noise scared people. Newspaper reporters teased Robert.

People in other countries were also building rockets. Germany was one of those countries. It was like a race. Who would make the best rocket first? Robert did not want to give up.

Charles Lindbergh, a famous pilot, read the newspaper stories about Robert's exploding rocket. He believed in Robert's research and helped him find money to continue his work.

Robert and Esther moved from Massachusetts to Roswell, New Mexico. Not

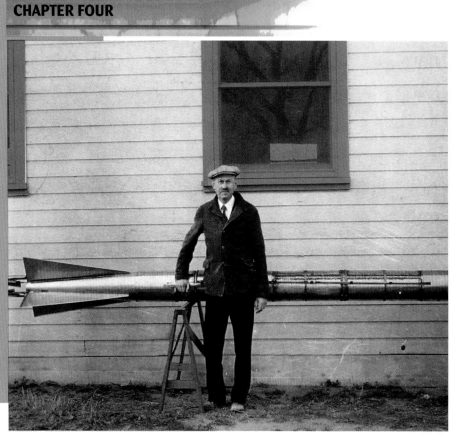

Esther took lots of pictures of Robert before he launched one of his rockets. Here Robert is about to launch a rocket in Roswell, New Mexico.

many people lived there, and the weather was usually sunny and clear. When Robert tested his rockets in Roswell, no one was scared.

On December 30, 1930, he tested a rocket that was 11 feet long and weighed 33 pounds. It flew two thousand feet into the sky. Its speed was 500 miles per hour. That was the highest and fastest rocket Robert had ever flown.

Along the way, Robert had to solve a lot of problems to improve his rockets. For example, some of the rockets got too hot. He invented a way to cool them by spraying liquid on them from the inside. Robert called this his curtain cooling system. He also invented a way to help steer the rockets.

Robert did not want anyone to copy his rockets, so he took out **patents** (PAT-unts). Patents protect an inventor by making it against the law for anyone to copy an invention without permission. But Robert still worried.

In May 1935, one of his rockets flew over seven thousand feet high. In 1937, one flew

Robert and his crew examine a rocket that was launched in New Mexico.

over eight thousand feet into the air. That is more than a mile and a half. But it was still far from outer space.

Robert (second from left) and three of his assistants are very proud of their rocket.

WORLD WAR II AND FINAL YEARS

Robert worked with just a small crew of people. Other scientists wanted to help. Robert said no.

In 1939, World War II started. In 1941, the United States joined other countries that were fighting in the war. Robert wanted to help America.

The U.S. Navy asked Robert for help. Robert agreed.

He worked on jet engines. It was dangerous for everyone involved. When one person almost died during an experiment, the work stopped. Robert helped the U.S. Navy with other research projects instead.

Robert is famous all over the world. Here is a wax statue of him at the Goddard Space Flight Visitor Center in Greenbelt, Maryland.

Germany was also in the war. They fought the United States, England, and several other countries. Germany attacked England with **V-1 and V-2 rockets**. Robert examined a V-2. It had many of the same systems as his rockets. Had Germany copied Robert's rockets?

Near the end of the war, Robert got sick. He could not talk, so he wrote notes. People tried reading them, but his writing was not very neat. Instead, Robert tried using Morse code, a tapping code developed for the telegraph system. Telegraphs are messages sent over wires using tapping sounds.

In June 1945 the doctors told Robert he had throat cancer. They operated, but it did not help. Robert died on August 10, just a few weeks before the war ended.

Esther was sad. She talked about Robert and his work. People realized Robert had been a great scientist. Many years after he died, they awarded him medals. The Goddard Space Flight Center in Greenbelt, Maryland, was named after him.

This is the NASA-Goddard Space Flight Center in Greenbelt, Maryland. It is dedicated to Robert Goddard and his rockets.

Astronauts have flown into Earth orbit and to the moon. Rockets have taken them there. Rockets have launched satellites into space. Someday rockets will take astronauts to other planets.

Robert Goddard was right about rockets. They are useful for traveling into outer space.

He really was a Rocket Man.

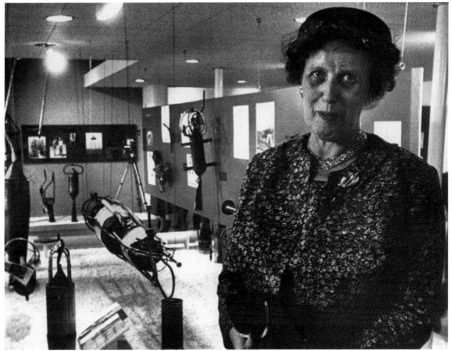

Robert's wife, Esther, about age 58.

CHRONOLOGY

1882 Born on October 5 in Worcester, Massachusetts

1898 Reads *War of the Worlds* by H. G. Wells

1899 Decides to build a rocket while trimming a cherry tree

1913 Gets very sick and doctors expect him to die, but gets better

1919 Writes that rockets could someday reach the moon

1924 Marries Esther Kisk on June 21

1926 First flight of a liquid fuel rocket is made on March 16

1930 Moves to Roswell, New Mexico, to test rockets

1937 Tests a rocket that flies over eight thousand feet high, his highest ever

1945 Dies on August 10

Books

Farley, Karin Clafford. *Robert H. Goddard.* Englewood Cliffs, N.J.: Silver Burdett Press, 1991.

Maurer, Richard. *Rocket! How a Toy Launched the Space Age.* New York: Crown Publishers, 1995.

Quackenbush, Robert. *The Boy Who Dreamed of Rockets: How Robert Goddard Became the Father of the Space Age.* New York: Parents Magazine Press, 1978.

Streissguth, Thomas. *Rocket Man: The Story of Robert Goddard.* Minneapolis: Carolrhoda Books, Inc, 1995.

Verral, Charles Spain. *Rocket Genius.* New York: Scholastic Book Services, 1963.

Web Addresses

Clark University, Dr. Robert H. Goddard Web Pages
http://www.clarku.edu/offices/library/archives/Goddard.htm

National Inventors Hall of Fame, Inventor Profile
http://www.invent.org/hall_of_fame/67.html

World Almanac For Kids, "Robert Hutchings Goddard"
http://www.worldalmanacforkids.com/explore/inventions/goddard_roberth.html

Roswell Visitors Bureau, "Robert Hutchings Goddard"
www.roswellcvb.com/goddard.html

GLOSSARY

engineer (en-juh-NEER) a person who knows how to use engines or machines

fuel (FYOO-el) something that powers something else

Martian (MAR-shun) a creature who lives on Mars

Tuberculosis (too-BUR-kya-LOW-sis) a disease that affects lungs

V1/V2 rockets (rock-ITS) special bombs made by Germany in World War II

satellite (sat-UH-lite) something that revolves around a planet in outer space

INDEX

Anniversary Day 7

British 15

Chinese 15

Earth 9, 15

England 27

Germany 19, 27

Goddard, Robert
    birth of 9
    death of 27
    parents of 9
    sicknesses of 9, 11, 13, 27

Goddard Space Flight Center 27

Kisk, Esther 17, 19, 27

Lindbergh, Charles 19

Mars 5

Martians 9

Massachusetts 19

Morse Code 27

New Mexico 19

Navy, U.S. 25

United States 25, 27

Wells, H.G 9

Worcester 9

World War I 15

World War II 25